death will come

Bill Denham

Fernwood
PRESS

death will come

Fernwood Press
Newberg, Oregon
www.fernwoodpress.com

Printed in the United States of America

"Matt's Funeral" appeared in *Looking for Matthew*.

Cover photograph: Benjaminrobyn Jespersen
Author photograph: Elvira Linda Piedra

ISBN 978-1-59498-044-2

This book is dedicated to all the children in my life—

natural, adopted and otherwise.

Contents

The old man

He is an old man
    whose heart has suffered blows.
    Like an ancient locket,
    lost beneath the rubble
    bombs had left,
    where shattered walls
    dropped giant beams like pickup sticks,
    its precious metal misshapen, now,
    bent, battered beyond repair,
    unable to close again,
    this old heart sprung open so
    lets the soft flame of its suffering out—
    that it might blend and mix with others'
    to make a larger light
    against the darkness.

Death will come

We think now of death—
  not with fear—
  with interest,
  knowing we will be gone,
  not knowing how we will live on
  in the hearts and souls of those we've touched,
  not just for good but for ill, as well.

We think of those we've lost,
  both to death and to life,
  and know they are in us still, inside of us—
  make of us, in straight and twisted ways
  who we have come to be—
  their coercion and their embrace.

So ask me how that works
  or how I know these things
  and I'll likely shrug,
  raise my brows,
  offer my open palms spread wide.
  There's the mystery.

Yet, I do remember things—
    Nancy's laugh, her stories,
    her eyes, her face when she took me
    into her immeasurable heart—held me
    always in that special place, amidst the throng;
    Matthew's soft mask, his infectious smile
    that spoke his gentleness and hid his pain;
    my first born—Barbara's anguished cry,
    across an old land line—
    You are not the Dad, I know—
    and understand, in time, her pain
    and hold the love I had and thought and tried to give;
    my second born—Helen's fierce, detached and icy logic,
    laying into me about her mother's needs,
    not knowing, yet, her own
    nor how I had fathered her, imperfectly;
    her mother's pain,
    tempestuous, explosive rage,
    endless analysis, breathtaking projection—
    decades, decades till I began to see my part;
    my mother's needs,
    gifted in subtle and not so subtle ways to me—
    her beauty, a certain love, honesty and industriousness;
    my father's wartime absence,

his distance upon return—"Hey, Billy, come here.
Look at this."—never a connection in that way—
not that I remember—before his angering,
unexpected death as I turned fourteen—
yet I hear still the beauty and the rhythms of his voice,
his public voice absorbed each Sunday for near a decade,
I know his steadfastness, his uprightness, his belief—his
    love.

Such are the familiar refrains
    for those who know me
    and there are other losses I could list
    but when I think, now, of my own departure
    I cannot say how or if I will live on,
    even with the hedge of all my words scattered among
        friends.

So nothing's different as death comes closer
    or as we think that death comes closer, as we age,
    for, in fact, it is with us, always, from the beginning.
    I know that.
    I've been told I was near death at the beginning
    and near two and a half decades out from that Sunday
        morning brush in '41
    I came closer still on Cedar Street in Berkeley,
    sailing over my handlebars and into the windshield

of an auto that had turned in front of me,
severing my jugular and exposing my aorta—
sure death without the firm hand of Robert Lane,
visiting prof from Yale, stuffed into my near-severed
   neck
and held there till help arrived.

So thinking of death or not,
   thinking of how we will be remembered or not
   thinking honestly, if we can, of our impact for good or
      for ill or not
   changes nothing, really, for life is what it is, regardless,
      always a gift
   and how we use it is always a choice,
   whether our hearts are big enough to hold multitudes
   or whether they still hide secrets from ourselves.
   Even so, I do think of death.
   I do wonder how I will live on
   inside of those I've touched.
   What of me lost? What part passed on,
   informing, even another generation?

And what of the time yesterday morning
   with tiny Illiana at the studio
   responding to her calls,
   Bill, I need more paper.

Bill, I need another cracker,
or dismantling the large wooden paper pallet
with pry bar and with hammer,
handing her the nails, one by one,
which she expectantly received
and proudly held in her tiny hand,
counting, as she knew one does with such things,
in her own inimitable, confident, yet incorrect way,
or walking the sidewalk and hallways,
at the Calou building, her younger sister, Amelia,
slung across my forearm, belly down,
as she would not be comforted on my shoulder,
comforted, instead, by looking out at the world
and watching her older sister skip happily ahead of us,
while mom crunched the numbers with a client—
just one of a million moments—
not entirely unlike the hundreds or thousands
such moments spent with Barbara and Helen,
or with Terry, Kate, Cary, John and Matthew,
Rachel, Charlotte, Rosie and Leslie
or with Eli, or Ciara and Kaelin?
Who knows, really?
I don't.

I do know, I am, at once, the same as ever
        and entirely different from those earlier years.
        I do know near seventy years
        has made a difference
        in what I know of myself
        and as far as this morning goes,
        I wouldn't do it different than I did.
        I am sure of that.
        Beyond that?
        I don't
        know.

I do know
        when my sweet love
        called from Portland this morning
        and we shared a few minutes
        talking about life, the way we do,
        she said to me—and I don't need to give you the
                details—
        Sometimes we simply allow the moment to be the
                abundance!

Nancy –

October 28, 1937–March 25, 2007

Nancy Varney Adamson and I
    shared a serendipitous connection—
    the same birth day, October 28th,
    but our connection went well beyond
    the serendipitous,
    to the very edge
    of what it means
    to be a human being—
    at least for me.

I knew not her shadow.
    She knew her own
    and held that close to herself,
    more than most of us
    are able to do—I think.
    I knew her by her light
    and in my particular case
    that light, her light,
    in all its mystery
    helped illuminate
    a terrible darkness
    in my life,

let me see, so to speak,
where it was my feet
needed to take me—
amazing grace
to be so
touched
by another.

Godspeed, dear, dear Nancy.

Life's ledger

To have lost you,
    the way I have lost you,
    is a most terrible pain
    and hardly bearable.
    So I rarely go there,
    though you are a permanent part
    of me (and I of you).
    But sometimes, a particular conversation,
    or a particular experience
    with loved ones,
    throws me, unexpectedly,
    into that mysterious place
    we inhabit together—
    to this day, to this very moment—
    suddenly there are floods,
    suddenly there are explosions,
    suddenly nothing is ordinary.
    Gaining myself
    has come at
    a great cost—
    yet I am here,
    openhearted.

Matt's funeral

You know what I hate about funerals?
    Well, there are lots of things,
    but I'll start with preachers
    who think they can offer consolation
    by slamming Islam, Judaism and Buddhism,
    as if that had anything to do with Matthew.

I console myself by remembering Matthew,
    which is what everybody else was doing there
    and the stories were all the same,
    all two hours of them, coming from black people,
    brown people, white people, well-off people,
    poor people on the edge,
    ex-cons and homies, work buddies,
    sisters-in-law and aunties—
    not officially, not legally, understand,
    for Matt didn't marry Hazel or Hakiti
    the mothers of Jayvion and Makai.
    But that didn't matter—not here, not now.

And some of those stories were more real,
    more honest, than others,
    but nobody was like the preacher—
    even the auntie, who was struggling
    with her grief by talking Jesus talk.
    She was hurting, no hiding that,

and felt that terrible loss of connection.
That's what all the stories were about—connection.
Everyone there felt connected to Matthew.

There was no more beautiful smile in the universe
    than Matt's smile—once you saw that smile
    you were done, it was over, he was in your heart
    and that smile came from inside, from somewhere real,
    and that smile was on the face of a young man
    who had been dealt a crummy hand.

I know. I know the whole story.
    And it was inspirational to hear each person
    speak of how Matt had touched their lives,
    and how they had borne witness to all his efforts
    to turn his life around and to his love
    for Jayvion and Makai.
    I know the back story,
    the parts they didn't say
    and that's ok. I'll give them that.
    It wasn't a white wash. It was real,
    and I knew, as I listened, me and Matt, we're alike,
    the way that works with your children, sometimes—
    when we can see ourselves in them and they in us
    and sometimes that's a joy,
    sometimes a sadness,
    a cause for grief.

But Matt—Matt was hope
in the midst of hopelessness.
He was smiling and laughing
with his friends when he was shot,
from behind—one bullet to the head, one to the back—
by two masked kids in an act of retaliation
or initiation—who knows what?
Maybe some kind of turf war,
right here, not halfway 'round the world
in Afghanistan or Iraq—right here.

So when I spoke of Matt, that evening,
I spoke of that hope,
but you should know I only said a part
of what was on my mind—the other part,
the part I played in his upbringing—those mistakes,
the owning of which allowed for hope
but could not erase, in so short a time, if ever,
the limits laid down on the life of this child—
I carried that part with me as I left the mortuary
with my son, Leslie, and his friend.
It went unspoken,
but I carry it and I will carry it
each minute of every day.
What I do with that is on me.
There is no helping Matthew, now.
There is only remembering him.

A wondering . . .

There is a certain lack of affect
    I see, sometimes, in soldiers
    back among us,
    telling us their tales of war,
    and I wonder, as I watch,
    if they are not unlike me,
    unable, most often, to weep
    for what we've done—
    though I am no veteran
    of their kind of war
    I have done deeds
    for which I need
    to weep
    and yet I find
    my fear does not allow
    my tears to fall—my fear
    that I may in some unknowing way
    be indulging myself in pity.
    And I cannot abide self-pity
    nor anyone who hides
    what's theirs to own
    behind such tears—
    which feeling strikes me
    as quite a marshal one—

and so I wonder, still,
if we are not brothers
in that way, as well
as in all the others.

Paradise Lost

for Barbara

Part I

1.

Barbara, my first born,
    you are so sadly a stranger to me,
    though I nurtured you well
    when you were small.

It's not a conscious memory, I know,
    but when your mother left you in my care
    to go looking for herself
    in the Haight
    and you would wake up,
    tiny as you were,
    I would place you
    gently on my lap
    and read to you aloud
    the words I loved,
    Paradise Lost.

You seemed to love them, too,
    for you sat so calmly
    on my lap,
    night after night,
    'til we'd read
    the whole book through

    2.

So, Barbara, from that early, early time
    of closeness and of bonding
    how have we now come,
    father and daughter,
    to be such strangers?

    I do know the answer—
    that is, as much as we can
    know the answers to such questions,
    and I'm learning all the time;
    but when I think of answering
    my own question,
    a deep despair settles over me.
    Yet I must go on.
    I must go on.
    I must.

When I say, "I know the answer,"
     I don't mean I know all the details—
     all the tiny, infinitesimal details,
     the daily events that unfolded
     over the years—largely in darkness
     and hidden from my view,
     no, not always hidden from my view
     but rather from my understanding—
     all the events that led inexorably
     to our separation,
     our alienation
     and our loss.

And I don't know that I can point
     to a single event
     or a specific time
     and say, "That's it!
     That's what triggered it
     or that's where it started."
     But I do remember, Barbara,
     and I have to share with you
     before it's too late.
     Is it too late?

3.

So let me tell you my story, Barbara,
    knowing it is my story, my truth,
    knowing, as well, if we are ever
    to reconcile, you and I,
    if our early bond is to be restored,
    if we are ever able
    to embrace once more,
    then you must hear—
    you must hear
    my story
    and I
    must
    hear
    yours,
    and know
    your truth.

Part II

Just days after Nelson Mandela walked free
    from Victor Verster prison,
    in the very center of our living room
    where I had watched him walk to freedom,
    I stood transfixed,
    frozen in the headlights
    of approaching disaster,
    feeling absolutely alone,
    knowing, deep in my heart,
    it was all over—
    holding the receiver
    at some distance from my ear,
    yet hearing clearly
    the passionate intensity
    in her voice, her command:
    "Get out of that house,"
    her order to walk away from
    my newly chosen family,
    to walk away from Ruth
    and from Rosie, our new
    and precious daughter.

Her words were clear;
       her rage not contained;
       her threat absolute and explicit.
       "You leave that woman
       or you will lose all
       your other children!"

I can't point to this moment and say
       it caused our separation, Barbara,
       for that took, at the very least,
       several lifetimes to arrive—
       not just yours and mine
       but your mother's, too,
       and your grandmothers'
       and your grandfathers',
       and on and on.

But I can look back, now, and see myself,
       in that place, at that time,
       and know it was there—
       my struggle to live began,
       for there was absolutely no way
       I could see your mother's words as loving—
       (though it was years before I knew that).

As her words ripped through me that day
like shrapnel,
I knew I would follow
her command—
my sense of self so faint,
my need for what she gave so great;
my choice was stark;
the math simple,
one or four?
I walked, that day,
away from freedom,
though the seeds
of my release
had been sewn.

Comice pears

Comice pears,
    ripe to the very edge of ripeness,
    are perhaps God's greatest gift,
    or so it seems when I slice one
    down the middle, quarter it, seed it
    and bite into its soft fullness
    and savor the sweet juices—
    some of which always, without fail,
    drip past my lips or down my fingers
    waiting, then, to be licked—
    that none of this gift
    might go unused.

If this, then, is God made flesh,
    who is Satan,
    if not my fear?

My Helen, my Iphigenia

Though years and years have passed
        since I have seen your face,
        I imagine your beauty
        remains undeniable,
        as it has always been,
        but in my heart,
        dear daughter,
        your story
        feels to me
        more that
        of Iphigenia
        than that of
        your namesake,
        and that, of course,
        is because I am your father.

The gods are cruel, aren't they?
        They often ask too much of us.

Way back, when you were hardly even a toddler,
   and we lived in faculty housing—
   those large, pale green, concrete blocks of buildings
   scrunched up against the dry,
   brush covered lava hillsides
   just leeward of Manoa valley—
   where tropical skies, tropical lushness made those
      tropical smells—
   I made a bed for your mother and me.
   (I was always making things—as still I am—
   that hasn't changed a bit.)
   The bed was a plywood slab, a foam pad
   and a frame—nothing special;
   but from the scraps—
   from the scraps
   I made some magic
   nesting blocks;
   do you remember the
   nesting blocks?

If I try very, very hard, I can almost remember
        how I did it, how I laid it out
        in my mind, and made the cuts
        and put it all together
        so they slid so neatly
        one into the other—
        all six of them—
        and then sat upside down
        in the corner of your room
        looking like an ordinary box,
        big enough to sit upon or stand upon
        or to be a little table for your play
        and no one would ever suspect,
        even for a minute,
        the secret it
        contained.

Remember those nesting blocks?
　　They traveled with us for years.
　　I made sure of that,
　　as if I were trying to hold on to something
　　each time we'd move;
　　and we were always moving,
　　even there in Hawaii, could never seem to stay
　　in one place for very long.
　　They died, finally, I think,
　　those nesting blocks, somehow,
　　up in that Appalachian hollow
　　when I could no longer keep things together,
　　things like nesting blocks—
　　for you
　　or for
　　me.

How many times when you were very small
        did I sing you to sleep,
        my hand resting upon your back
        moving your small body
        back and forth, back and forth
        in gentle, gentle motion
        until I could feel you
        let go beneath my touch,
        drift into your own world
        of dreams? Do you remember?
        I don't know the number
        but I do remember, Helen—
        I do remember.

No way now to tell of all the memories of you
        and of your sister and your brother
        in those early years—hundreds of them and so many,
            many more
        as our lives twisted and turned in unexpected
        and frequently disturbing and often confusing ways,
        as you grew toward womanhood.
        But I do remember things and I think my thoughts
        and sometimes curse myself, sometimes curse the gods,
        sometimes simply weep.

In the way we do, sometimes,

we adults, we tell stories to our children—

I can speak to you now this way

for though you are my child, you are all grown up,

accomplished, so I hear, and into your fifth decade.

These stories we tell our children, often as not,

have some fearful turn, like a fairytale—

this story, as a Russian matryoshka, nests inside our
story,

inside our parents' stories, inside their parents' stories

and so forth—not necessarily

knowing where we are

in our telling of this story

or that story to our child—

or to ourselves, for that matter,

the whys and the where it comes from

and the what it does for us.

And this, as I suggest, may be true

of any story we tell, is likely to be true,

and telling stories, of course,

is our most constant activity.

Having said all this, Helen, let me

tell you a story, "which, of course, is what I am already
doing."

So follow the thread, then, if you can—
or not—for sometimes, perhaps,
a story is only a story—
no matryoshka
nor baboushka—
perhaps—but this
is what came to mind.

When Hannah was a little girl
    her mother had told
    or read to her the story
    of a little boy named Jacob
    who was a good little boy,
    who helped his mother
    sell her vegetables at market
    but who had the misfortune to fall
    under the spell of a wicked witch
    who changed his appearance
    to that of a dwarf with a great long nose
    so that his parents could no longer recognize him.
    Hannah's mother thought to tease her daughter,
    calling her dwarf nose
    and pretending to not recognize
    her own flesh and blood.

As an adult, many years on,
    Hannah recalled vividly
    and viscerally the terror
    she had experienced at that moment
    as she cried out in anguish, in desperate panic to her
        mother,
    "No! I am Hannah! I am Hannah, your daughter!"

I can't say, Helen, all the reasons
    Hannah's haunting story came to mind.
    I know a few, and surely my loss of you
    and of your sister remains a white hot iron,
    not cooled by time—forcing a focus at my core,
    in my heart on the reasons why—
    beneath the giant live oak tree
    whose spreading limbs
    had arched upward at first
    from a trunk now grown so large
    that, were it felled, I could have
    laid my body out upon the stump
    and barely touched the edges,
    or so my memory tells me
    and we all know about memory, don't we—

there we set up shop, you and I,
our little cabinet shop,
beneath those oldest of limbs
that closest to the earth
now seemed drawn back there
and hung heavy with Spanish moss
and stretched wide across the sandy soil.

You shared a room with your two sisters—
one full, one half, a different dad
one older, one younger,
and I and your even younger still half-brother,
a different mom, had turned
the rec room into our home
and so we lived or thought to
and thought, as well, to make a desk together
for you and your young sister—
split-level like those modern houses
that seemed so strange to me when first I saw them—
an ordinary height for you,
for you were leaving childhood behind,
had done so already, but your young sister
was right in the middle of it and going off to school
and needed a level to fit her size.

And then we made a chair for her—
all painted white with Muppets on it, maybe
and that was, in whatever way it was,
a dad and daughter time—
the last such time
we shared—
I think—
unless my memory fails me
and as time moves
how short a time it was,
and how long a time, now,
has memory to stretch
across this quarter century.

Amidst this loss and sadness
    that lives where I live—always,
    even as I learn to love,
    as I am, from time to time, overcome by beauty or by joy
    as I go about my days making this and making that
    even as I hold within myself some simple sense of well
        being—

another memory comes, one that surfaces with some
        regularity—
as a recurring dream might, ready to rise,
resting, not deeply buried,
ready to give some gift to me,
as such memories or dreams
that come and come again
and again, always do.

This particular memory that comes so to me
        is of a story, a story that came from you
        and took place, your telling of it,
        your sharing it with me,
        beneath another tree,
        a dozen years on or more from our time beneath the
                giant live oak,
        no working together, now, side by side,
        no soft sandy soil beneath our feet
        but the hard and unforgiving concrete
        of a city sidewalk—
        the tree, this time, more vertical,
        less grand and less protective,
        yet giant in its own right
        and a giver of gifts, this Santa Rosa plum,
        whose gifts I took and turned to jams and jellies
        of a most exquisite kind, this Santa Rosa plum

that towered above the second floor of your mom's new
    house
where I, too, had lived these last few years
with all six of your half siblings,
a house I now felt compelled to leave.
And in my leaving, I spoke to you of why
and in so doing spoke critically of your mother
which I had not done as you grew up,
quite the opposite (but that's another part of my story)
and so my shocking words, no surprise,
called up from you, my second daughter,
a story of your mother's love.
The story goes,
if memory serves me right,
your mother's father had been mean to you
somewhere in your early double digits
and when your mother heard your story
of his mistreatment, she took time—
she took time with you
to slowly and carefully explain
who your grandfather, her father, was
so that you might better understand him,
and you felt from this moment together
your mother's love and told the story to me
in that way.

And I have learned, Helen, over time
    my own part in the creation of this story
    you shared with me, on that day,
    now so many years ago,
    this story that will not yet leave my memory
    nor should it do so
    until it has no more to teach me
    about the ways I am Agamemnon
    and you my Iphigenia,
    the ways we are the gods.
    Yet know, I do, dear Helen, Agamemnon,
    though he may know and feel everything,
    cannot speak his daughter's loss nor her sadness
    nor her anger nor her love—for only she can tell her
        story.

God

upon reading Rabbi Lerner's essay

When I look around,
    I do see inexplicable phenomena,
    a reality beyond the grasping
    a beauty beyond the telling
    a suffering beyond the holding
    and God does not come up, for me.
    It seems ok, simply to sit with the mystery
    and maybe tell a story, if one comes.

I don't mean to be judgmental or presumptuous
    or especially taken with myself in any way
    but I do observe the presence of God
    postulated in people's lives, in people's language
    that may as easily make them worse as make them
        better

probably more easily make them worse,

to my eyes and to my ears,

for this postulated god seems most always to be

an expression of some need—

some explanation or some justification or both

which reflect, to my eyes,

a seeming inability to sit with mystery,

to live as if there is no God,

to acknowledge our aloneness

to own our own lives—

the joy and the pain

we give and we receive

and to come, then, to the point of death,

the end of life, having passed nothing off,

and are so, fulfilled.

Beyond that?

I don't know.

Mom and me

My mother was spunky,
    a little fireplug of a woman
    who didn't move slowly,
    who carried her anxieties
    and resentments just below the surface
    and might break into song
    or begin whistling or bustling,
    doing any manner of things,
    just to keep that magma
    down.

She was beautiful
    to my little boy eyes
    and I'd say, as well,
    to the eyes of the world
    in that 1940s star-style way—
    the hair, the makeup, the dress—
    captured in black and white
    on that old folding-bellows Kodak
    whose slim-trim, black, art-deco body
    would open out like magic to take in the world—
    my world, my mother.

And she was at the center.
    She was mine, more than my brothers',
    more than my father's, even,
    in that mother-son kind of way
    that can sometimes happen
    and there was a certain sexual energy there.
    From my side, which is all I can really talk about, I
        suppose,
    it was there and I've told the story before
    of our encounter on the stairs
    when I was twelve and beginning
    to fill up with hormones.

And who knows the accuracy
    of those memories
    or of any memories, for that matter?
    But for me, more than half a century out,
    there's a palpable reality to the image
    of my mother's "slip-clad naked body/
    standing just feet from me."

Did it happen? Did she really say,
      "What are you looking at, Billy?"
      Well, whether it did or no, it is a part of me
      and certainly my connection with my mother,
      for good and for ill remains as central to my being
      as it was in 1947 when I walked, all by myself,
      a whole mile, all the way across town, to school,
      quite full of my six-year-old self,
      with that bounce in my step and just a-whistling
      or later on that day or maybe on another,
      when I held my hand high,
      trying desperately to catch the eye
      of Miss Margret Cruickshank
      to ask permission to go pee—
      unsuccessfully.

Gifts received and given

Bill Goodykoontz turned in his grave last night—
    for there I was near half a century out
    from our time together—our short, short time together
    in that most unlikely of places his flaming soul had
        found—
    not as a refuge, certainly, but as a place to pause—
    a Southern Presbyterian college
    in a small North Carolina town,
    where I had brought my own, young,
    unknown spirit ready to be ignited,
    ready to be ravished by the sounds
    and rhythms of the spoken word.
    And so it was in that place and at that time
    I heard from him the words of Jeffers
    and Yeats and Hopkins and Thomas.
    And though that flame ignited
    lay small and hidden even from myself
    for decades at a time it has been rekindled
    by another flaming soul and more than one.
    So last night, amongst these other flaming souls,
    in the very heart of San Francisco,
    bursting full and vibrant from my mouth
    came those late words of Robinson Jeffers

The deer lay down their bones—
these words laid down, given back as they must be
    given,
as they cannot avoid being given,
having once and forever been taken into my own heart
where now they live as fuel among the others
and inform my very being.
So there you see, now, dear listener,
why it is Bill Goodykoontz
turned in his grave last night.
Bless his soul.

Your half-smoked pack of *Camels*

Sometimes I wonder
  what went through your mind
  that day, or in that moment.
  Did you think of me?

You didn't come to dinner
  when Mom called.
  I remember the day,
  November 2nd, 1955.
  My watch had stopped
  at exactly 4:03 that afternoon,
  the watch you'd given me
  two years before,
  the one you'd brought back
  from the war.

Bob had gone to look for you
  and I had followed:
  out the back door,
  across the driveway,
  up the wooden steps,
  and into your study.

Then like my watch, time itself seemed to have stopped.
    I simply stood and stared,
    feeling ever so far away,
    seeing ever so clearly,
    as a hawk high above the earth,
    motionless on the wind,
    sees each small detail
    far below—

    grandpa's desk in the center,
    the one he had made,
    the single center drawer
    so orderly and filled with such treasures,
    your *black Smith Corona portable*
    on which you had typed
    so many sermons
    and practiced them aloud
    over and over and over,
    into the wee hours
    of the morning,
    as if you could not speak, directly,
    from your heart,
    the *half-smoked pack of Camels*
    beside your *polished brass ashtray*,
    made from a spent howitzer-shell
    and engraved by one of your buddies

(Did you have buddies?
Did chaplains have buddies?):
"145th Sea Bee Battalion"—Is that what it said?
I can't remember—exactly,
but I remember the rings on the bottom
and the little indentation in the center,
made when that shell was fired,
(Who fired it anyway? A buddy of yours?
And who was killed by it? Nobody?
I remember what you called them
in your letters home with little
cartoon drawings of coconuts
falling on their heads.
Who knew? Nobody?)
and I remember the handle:
straps, cut from the sides of the shell
and bent across the bowl,
each half growing thinner
till it met the other
at a polished braze-weld
in the center.

And when I looked at you, *Dad*,
　　I hated your *blue nails*,
　　your cold *swollen hands*
　　resting on the arms
　　of your *old easy chair*.
　　I hated you for just sitting there,
　　breathless, among your *books*
　　in the pale yellow light
　　cast through the *scalloped glass*
　　of the three *Gothic windows*
　　on your left.

I hated you, for leaving me, yet again.
　　I had seen you with my toddler's eyes,
　　looking up through
　　the lace embroidered
　　curtains of Grandmother
　　Lowrance's parlor doors.
　　All dressed up in your Navy blue uniform,
　　you bent down and pulled her small frame
　　close to you in a last parting embrace.
　　Then like a segue in an old silent movie
　　you faded out and were gone.

You did come back, after the war,
when I was only four
but you were not there
and I had dreamed for years we'd talk
when I was a grown-up too.

But on that day, November 2nd, 1955, you left
your *half-smoked pack of Camels*
and me behind. And sometimes
I wonder what went through your mind
that day or in that moment.
Did you know you were dying?
Did you know you were leaving me?
Was my dream your dream, too?
Were you also waiting to talk?

My father's gift

I remember hearing my father's voice
    from beyond the grave.
    No dream—a single, scratchy vinyl
    had captured his characteristic
    lilting, homiletic style,
    that seemed,
    in and of itself,
    to be the message—
    no surprises there,
    nor flights,
    yet a resonance
    that touched
    and stays with me
    a half a century later,
    informing
    my very
    own.

Tornadoes

Not all tornadoes
    rip and ravage wide swaths
    across grasslands, the flat prairies
    nor deep into the wet pungent air
    of old plantation country.
    No! No Joplin nor Tuscaloosa, here.
      These drop,
      bomb-like
       from the
       turbulent
        skies of
        my mind,
        dip down
        randomly
        here and
        there and
        lay waste
        to all I
        have
        made
        for my
        self
        over
        the
        years—

those sturdy structures, carefully placed,
laboriously raised across the landscape of my soul—
my sanctuaries, my havens—
the places where I go to know
the peace of self acceptance.
Gone now!

And when those turbulent skies have cleared,
    I stand amidst the ruin and the rubble
    and I look up and I find distant points of light
    that tell me where I am
    and I know, then,
    I will build again
    a place for myself.

Carrying Ilianna

I could not say there was
    an immediate sense of well being—
    simply that I was doing what needed to be done—
    the child was in need,
    the mother unavoidably occupied,
    the others unable to quell the deep body sobs
    that shook her tiny self.

Speaking softly, reflecting in some way—
    I don't recall my words exactly—her distress,
    acknowledging it, as if I understood just how she felt,
    bending slowly down,
    not so to avoid tweaking my back,
    though I was mindful of that,
    as to express with my body the comfort it might hold;
    I picked her up, rested her little butt on my right
        forearm,
    gently held her small back with my left hand,
    and began quietly, rhythmically singing some wordless
        chant or other,
    which rhythm matched my careful steps
    and the pats upon her back
    of my left hand.

And so the sobbing stopped—
her tiny towhead resting on my shoulder,
her body molded into mine.

I could not say there was
    an immediate sense of well being—
    simply that I was doing what needed to be done—
    and so we passed the time, she and I,
    walking the rectangular corridors of the old Calou
        building,
    my voice echoing through the low hallways
    and off the bricks and saw-tooth ceiling of the atrium,
    her small head, on occasion, lifting up to look at this or
        that
    and dropping back again—relaxed, not yet asleep.

No thought to stop, for I knew somehow
    from some distant, deep place,
    deeper than the left shoulder ache,
    more and more, now, my constant companion, as I grow
        older,
    that sleep was the end point, the need of her tired body,
        her active spirit,
    that sleep, restorative sleep, must come for all to be well.

I cannot tell you the number, how many times
we made the circuit together
anymore than I could tell you the number of breaths I
took,
or the number of steps or the number of notes intoned.

I could not say there was
an immediate sense of well being—
simply that I was doing what needed to be done—
nor can I tell you entirely
how I knew what I knew that day
nor how the echoes played out inside of me—
my mother's son, my children's father—
but I can say to you, dear listener, with some assurance
that when sleep did come and I laid her tiny body down
I did begin to feel that sense of well being I have
referenced—
a sense that grows still as I consider the echoes inside of
me,
as I consider who I was and who I am—

I carried Iliana as my mother may have done,
carried her as I have carried my daughters and my sons,
yet carried her as who I am today,
the self, same as ever in many ways,
yet so much older now—children lost—
those deeper aches embraced and held,
seem to make each day anew,
to make me more nearly who
I may have been born to be
and there is a sense
of well being
that grows
in that.

Starry night

Were the gods to take
    all the moments of our lives
    and scatter them across the heavens
    like stars, for all to see,
    could we bear the beauty
    and the majesty and the mystery
    of our ordinary being, made visible so?
    Could we?

And could we then approach
    holding the invisible, as, also, a part of ourselves,
    the insatiable black holes that devour
    the very light of our lives,
    suck it down
    out of sight?
    Could we?

Epilogue

Dear daughters, I suffer
    the loss of you.
    I cannot tell
    which hurts the more
    on this rack of grief
    that stretches my soul
    near to the breaking point,
    ripping sinew from bone—
    the desolation of loss
    or the knowing
    you are most likely
    unable to know and feel
    your own,
    for though my love for you
    was and is profound,
    flesh of my flesh,
    spirit of my spirit,

I taught you too well
how not to know
your own soul.
I grieve that error
and pray forgiveness
and hold myself
in the light of
that knowing
and rejoice
in that light.

Bill Denham

Bill was educated in the South at Davidson College and at UC Berkeley in the mid-sixties where he received his MA in English Literature. He rejected a promising academic career after five years of teaching at Luther College and the University of Hawaii to go back to the land in the mountains of West Virginia. Bill's subsequent journey of self-discovery has been turbulent, painful, and ultimately rewarding.

Now in his mid-70s, Bill is a retired letterpress printer from Painted Tongue Press in Oakland, California, where his collection of intricate paper sculptures still hang from the ceiling. He relocated to Portland, Oregon, to be with an old high school classmate, June Quackenbush, whom he married on December 27, 2013, after they reconnected at their 50th high school reunion in September of 2009 in Winston-Salem, North Carolina.

Bill has been writing poetry since the year 2000 and has published two small volumes. In 2013, the Apocryphile Press in Berkeley, California, published, *Looking for Matthew*—seventeen lyric and narrative poems that explore Bill's grief and responsibility following the street slaying of

Matthew Avery Solomon on September 4, 2008. In 2016, Finishing Line Press, Georgetown, Kentucky, published *Of gossamers and grace*—thirteen poems celebrating the mystery, the joys and sadnesses of Bill and June's late life love story. His poem, *Do you remember, Dad?*, appeared in the anthology, *Daring to Repair* (Wising Up Press, 2012). Other poems have been shared widely among friends and colleagues at poetry salons and spoken-word events and have appeared online over the years, primarily in his postings, *More morning musings from the land of the open heart*, through the listserve for The Redwood Men's Center, Sebastopol, California (redwoodmen.org).